# IN THE COUNTRY

Translated by Charles Lynn Clark

Printed in France

© Fernand Hazan, Paris, 1986.
ISBN : 2 85025 115 1

# IN THE COUNTRY

Sylvie Patin
Curator, Musée d'Orsay, Paris

ÉDITIONS HAZAN
RÉUNION DES MUSÉES NATIONAUX

" It was autumn. On both sides of the path, the harvested fields stretched off into the distance, golden with the stubble of oats and the cut wheat still lying on the ground...

" At last, the sun came up before us, a red ball on the horizon ; and, as it rose, growing brighter by the minute, the countryside seemed to awake and smile, then stretch and, like a girl just out of bed, remove its diaphanous white nightgown.

" ...What one loves most about these aimless walks is the countryside... the woods, the rising sun, the dusk, the moonlight. For painters, walks are honeymoons with the earth. During these long tranquil expeditions, they are alone with their beloved. They can lie down in a prairie, brimming with daisies and poppies, and, warmed by the sun's radiance, contemplate a tiny village in the distance as its steeple's bells ring out that it is noon... "

Maupassant, *Miss Harriet,* 1884

*D*uring the latter half of the nineteenth century, French landscape painting — from the Barbizon School to the movements that sprang up in the 1880s and 1890s (Pointillism, Pont Aven, Symbolism, and the Nabis) — underwent profound changes ; the most famous movement of them all, the movement whose official birth in 1874 provoked a veritable scandal, was, of course, Impressionism. The Musée d'Orsay could be called a "landscape museum " ; for, its rich collections fully retrace the long evolution of French landscape painting in the last century. Thanks to the diversity of its acquisitions and, moreover, to the generosity of certain great collectors, the museum houses collections that make it possible to study landscape and, in particular, the different faces of the French countryside of yesteryear in an absolutely unique way. The decisive rupture that occurred in landscape painting in the mid-nineteenth century is clearly visible in the museum's collections, which show how landscape ceased to be a mere background or setting to become the subject of the picture, treated in and for itself, as painters began to grapple with the insertion of the human figure in the landscape.

# THE BARBIZON PAINTERS AND THEIR INFLUENCE

*A* group of painters abandoned both the Classical principles of the historical landscape and the picturesque aspect of the Romantic landscape in favor of a vision that was closer to nature. These artists escaped from Paris to the Forest of Fontainebleau, where they adopted the villages of Marlotte, Chailly-en-Bière, and Barbizon. Far from city life, they laid the foundations of the Barbizon School and, so doing, influenced French landscape painting in a lasting way ; guided by their concern for truthfulness, they sought to enter into direct contact with nature ; and, in order to represent the diversity of country life as truly as possible, they studied the peasants working in the fields and forests (ill. 12, Millet, *The Gleaners*) or, in some cases, animal life (especially Troyon, Daubigny, and Rosa Bonheur ; ill. 2, 8).

Monet, Renoir, Sisley, and Bazille were also refusing academic convention when they left their teacher Gleyre's studio in 1863 and set out for an inn called the Cheval-Blanc at Chailly-en-Bière. In retrospect, the most significant thing about the period the future " Impressionists " spent studying in a Paris studio was not so much the traditional — and quite restricting — instruction they received there as the very fact of their meeting each other. The four friends' early works reveal their debt to their predecessors ; for, in their first attempts, they affirmed the same ideal of simplicity that the naturalist painters of the Barbizon School espoused. Like the Barbizon painters, they had studied the great English landscape painters (Benington, Constable, Turner) : the years he spent in England from 1857 to 1861 had allowed Sisley to discover the English artists at first hand ; and, Monet and Pissarro had sejourned in London at the time of the Franco-Prussian War and the Commune. Very popular on the English side of the Channel, the watercolor technique had contributed to bringing a new liberty to painting.

During the 1860s, following the example of the Barbizon painters, the new generation (Manet, Pissarro, Monet, Renoir, Sisley, Cézanne) continued to submit works to the yearly Salon, and certainly did not think it beneath them to have their paintings displayed in that forum of official art. Yet, if the Impressionists recognized their ties to the past, and sometimes even borrowed techniques used by such Barbizon painters as Courbet (his use of the palette knife) and Daubigny, they differentiated themselves from these artists by putting less emotion in their works and suppressing all "Romantic" touches from their landscapes, thus creating an objectivity which, up to that time, had only been seen in certain sketches painted directly from nature.

### THE CHOICE OF NEW SITES:
### THE IMPORTANCE OF TRANSPORTATION

*A*t first, the future Impressionists showed an almost filial sense of loyalty to the sites their predecessors preferred : they set out for the Forest of Fontainebleau, with the neighboring villages of Barbizon, Marlotte (where *mère* Anthony's inn was located), and Chailly-en-Bière, and for Normandy, with Trouville, Honfleur, and the famous Saint-Siméon abbey, one of the Barbizon painters' favorite haunts (see Chapter V).

But, they soon went their own way, abandoning the yearly Salon (although some of them did continue to be admitted) to display their paintings in "Impressionist" exhibitions (eight were held between 1874 and 1886) and one-man shows (often at the Galeries Durand-Ruel) ; at the same time, they opted for new sites that they felt were more in keeping with the spirit of their new age. A site's distance from Paris was a determinant element in its being chosen ; indeed, it is no exaggeration to say that distance was a key factor in the evolution of landscape painting in the second half of the nineteenth century. The French tranportation network, on water as well as land, had developed considerably ; moreover, new and rapid means of locomotion such as the steamboat and, especially, the train had made it possible for city dwellers to get out of town and spend a little time in surrounding countryside or "the suburbs". "In summer," Léon Say observed in his article on railroad travel in the 1867 *Paris-Guide*, "Parisians head out of town on trips that vary anywhere from four to fifty kilometers. The distance of these trips to the suburbs is determined by time and price."

Like the travelers of their day, the 1870 painters preferred places near the capital that could be reached easily. They were thus quite dependent on the French transportation system : the sites they chose, situated either along the railway lines or the Seine, corresponded exactly to the transportation routes and means of locomotion available to nineteenth-century Parisians. The young artists were first attracted to the region around Bougival, Chatou, Louveciennes, and Marly-le-Roi. Then, largely as a result of the Franco-Prussian War and the Commune, the painters separated and took their easels elsewhere : in December, 1871, Monet settled in

Argenteuil, while Pissarro, on his return from England, chose Pontoise and Auvers-sur-Oise, where Cézanne also lived for a time. Sisley was the artist who remained loyal longest to the region where Impressionism was born. Renoir divided his time among all of these places, sometimes painting at Monet's side, sometimes with Sisley.

The discovery of the French countryside, as reflected in the predominance of rural landscape painting in the second half of the last century (at the expense of " heroic " or " historical " landscapes painted in the studio), was not unrelated to a surge of nationalism among the French. Guidebooks were written describing France's most beautiful sites and indicating the most scenic views ; and, numerous city dwellers took their advice as, guidebooks in hand, they followed Frédéric Moreau and Rosanette through the Forest of Fontainebleau (Flaubert, *L'Éducation sentimentale,* 1869).

## THE APPEARANCE OF NEW MOTIFS IN LANDSCAPE PAINTING : IMAGES OF TRADITION AND MODERNITY

*T*he Impressionists did more than simply take advantage of the newly developed transportation network to reach their sites : they introduced images of that network into their works, finding motifs in it that they deemed just as worthy of their brushes as houses, farms, and mills... French and Italian painters had traditionally used roads to create an illusion of three-dimensionality in their compositions ; moreover, the seventeenth-century Dutch masters had considered roads as a motif in themselves. Their example was followed by the Impressionists who, far from simply depicting the countryside or the new, expanding " suburbs " and the various leisure activities found there, constantly represented the means of locomotion that allowed these areas to be reached. Several canvases illustrate the Impressionistic tribute to industrialization with particular brio : one of these is Monet's *Train in the Countryside* (ill. 43), with its holiday-bound passengers carefully silhouetted against the sky. A favorite spot of the artist's was the *Railroad Bridge at Argenteuil* where, like Renoir at the *Railroad Bridge at Chatou* (ill. 44), he was wont to linger before his easel.

Due to the importance they accorded roads (ill. 32, 33, 34, 35), railways, rivers and bridges, and the various corresponding modes of locomotion (carts, carriages, trains, boats...), the Impressionists were able to create a new iconography of landscape, the "ameliorated landscape" of their new industrial age. But, their contemporaries, apart from several particularly discerning critics like Zola, frequently saw nothing in their canvases but trivial subjects and retained only the visual shock created by the Impressionists' completely new technique and style. The Impressionist canvases are, in fact, much more complex than their apparent simplicity might lead one to believe. Far from being indifferent, the Impressionists chose their motifs with great care : in their landscapes, they balanced a traditional image of France with new elements linked to the industrial progress that was modernizing the face of the French landscape and, thereby, introduced "modernity" into painting. If the return to nature proned by the Barbizon School appealed to the Impressionists, as it most certainly did, they did not interpret it as implying a fanatical opposition to the industrialization and modernization of their nation ; on the contrary, they often found beauty in man's transformation of the landscape. In their own way, they were helping to celebrate the reconstruction of France that followed the ravages caused by the Franco-Prussian War (the building of new bridges, roads, etc.) ; while retaining a part of the heritage they had received from their predecessors, who painted virgin forests and quaint old mills and farms, they did not hesitate to place these traditional motifs next to factories and other signs of modernity in order to give as complete a vision as possible of their land.

## VARIOUS INTERPRETATIONS OF THE FRENCH COUNTRYSIDE IN PAINTING

Some of the Impressionists tended to look back to the past while others proved to be more attracted to the theme of progress. In both cases, however, the different sites chosen by the painters influenced their work and, thereby, the image they have left us of the French countryside of their day.

The Impressionist most attached to the countryside and the representation of rural or village landscapes was Pissarro, who, paradoxically enough, can also be considered a master of "urban landscape." Emphasizing the economic, industrial, and commercial aspects of the transportation network, he was led to prefer Pontoise and the surrounding region with the peasants who lived there (see

Chapter II). Yet, although he was interested in the recent invention of the railroad, the artist gave an old-fashioned, traditional vision of a countryside criss-crossed by carts and horses on dirt roads (ill. 24). In his "rustic" compositions, he often depicted peasants at work, and refused any and all allusions to modernity, preferring to show French farming in its most traditional forms: in fact, in their rural landscapes, all of the Impressionists tended to represent a timeless countryside, uneffected by the advances in agricultural technology then underway, thus adopting an attitude diametrically opposed to their treatment of the transportation theme. Pissarro's landscapes are peopled, as are Sisley's views of little Ile-de-France villages (ill. 30,40): numerous details evoke a human presence in these paintings which are, in this sense, just the opposite of Cézanne's deserted landscapes (ill. 20, 21, 28).

The countryside seen in Pissarro and Cézanne is cultivated and controlled by man (ill. 63, 65); both artists were drawn to the *Grainstacks* theme, as were Gauguin and the post-Impressionists (ill. 64, 66). Monet and Renoir were known to set up their easels out in the countryside around Argenteuil (ill. 51, 52); but, they also did more "artificial" pictures that reflect the popularity of "country outings" to the environs of Paris (for example, the popular La Grenouillère, located between Bougival and Chatou). In December, 1871, Monet moved to Argenteuil, a resort town then evolving into a modern "suburb," and invited Renoir and Sisley to join him. Monet and Renoir were particularly interested in representing the banks of the Seine as a place especially suited to the leisure activities of the Parisian bourgeoisie: joined by Caillebotte, they were frequently found painting at the Argenteuil Basin.

Finally, some of the Impressionists exploited the success the science and art of horticulture enjoyed from the 1850s to the 1890s. Amateur gardening gave rise to the publication of guidebooks written by the gardeners themselves; their gardens, which provided colorful motifs rich in contrasts of light and shade, could not but appeal to the plein-air painters. "In the nineteenth century... we find no painters specialized in representing gardens, though nearly all of them, at one time or another in their career, painted their own garden, or a friend's or teacher's" (Louis Vauxcelles). More than vegetable or "utility" gardens (which were, however, represented by Pissarro; ill. 26-27), the Impressionists were attracted to "pleasure gardens": Monet painted them at Sainte-Adresse (ill. 56), Argenteuil (ill. 49, 50), and then Giverny (ill. 78), Bazille on the terrace of his family's terrace in Méric (*Family Reunion*), and Pissarro at Pontoise (*Corner of the Garden at the Hermitage*). The two painters who proved to be most devoted to this subject were Monet and Caillebotte. The highly ornamental gardens at Argenteuil, so "bourgeois" in appearance, sometimes almost seem to be an insertion of town into country.

In addition to the use of new sites and motifs, and, of course, their particularly original technique based on the fragmentation of brushstroke and tone, the Impressionists also introduced a new, heightened perception of light, which eventually became the real subject of their pictures.

## HOURS AND SEASONS: IMPRESSIONS OF LIGHT

"*T*he group is pursuing, with quite obvious individual variations, a common artistic goal: on a technical level, they are trying to capture the ample light of the out-of-doors; on the level of feeling, they are attempting to convey the vividness of first sensations," the critic Philippe Burty wrote in *La République française* immediately after the opening of the first Impressionist exhibition (August 16, 1874). Several days later, Castagnary said of these artists: "If we want to characterize them with a single word that sums up what they are doing, we will have to coin the new term 'Impressionists.'. They are 'Impressionists' in the sense that they render not a landscape, but rather the sensation produced by a landscape. This word has, in fact, already become a part of their vocabulary: in the catalogue, M. Monet's *Sunrise* is not called a *landscape*, but an *impression...*" (*Le Siècle*, April 29, 1874). Louis Leroy, a critic writing for *Le Charivari*, is usually credited with giving the movement its name.

The Impressionists represented the richness of the French countryside by showing how it was transformed by the changing seasons. The cold weather inspired the artists to do magnificent landscapes showing the effects of winter and snow on the countryside (ill. 42, 57). The snow theme often appealed to the Impressionists, because it allowed them the perfect opportunity to study light variations and play on all of the nuances of their palette: thanks to their use of the fragmented stroke, the ground is never uniformly white (or black if it is in the shade), but iridescent with bluish reflections. As winter changed to spring, the painters — like Maupassant (*Au Printemps*, 1881) — happily greeted the new season and the coming of the beautiful days that would chase away the harshness of winter: the winter canvases, so impregnated with serene sadness, were followed by verdant landscapes brimming with cheerful blossoms. Pissarro (ill. 26), Monet, and Sisley transposed onto canvas the wonderful gaiety of orchards in spring. As harvest time rolled around, Pissarro, when not in the Pontoise region, would go to his friend Piette's in Mayenne to paint scenes of life on the farm (ill. 63).

Besides the alternating seasons, the Impressionists followed the evolution of nature during the course of the day, hour by hour, from the early morning on a winter day (ill. 23) to the setting sun on a waning autumn day. In late summer, 1890, Monet set out to paint the effects of morning and evening light on grainstacks (ill. 65). With these different versions of a single motif, which he painted in varying atmospheric conditions, but without changing, or only slightly, the position of his easel, Monet represented the perpetual modification of an object in time, from hour to hour and season to season. He thus began his work on " series, " which he later continued in his *Poplars* and Rouen *Cathedrals*. His goal was to express the ephemerality of things ; motivated by his desire to render their " instantaneity, " he carefully observed the play of light and shade, analyzing not so much the object as its progressive transformations in the changing light of day. Focusing his attention on the air and light, i.e., on what lay between his eye and the chosen motif, he attempted to paint the impalpable.

The titles under which the Impressionists' works were displayed in exhibitions reveal how much more important color, season, and time often were than place (for example, Pissarro's *Red Roofs, Corner of a Village in Winter*, ill. 25). The Impressionists' country landscapes are, for that matter, usually of scant topographical interest : they represent, above all, the constantly renewed richness of the French earth, as expressed in the country's fields and orchards or in man's efforts to dominate the land through agriculture, rather than any particular region. In this sense, they offer greater mythical value than do representations of cities, suburbs, and villages identified by explicit titles. This kind of symbolic meaning is at its greatest in Monet's spectacular series of *Grainstacks*.

## FURTHER INVESTIGATIONS : A NEW ERA BEGINS

*A*s the century drew to a close, the painters showed an increasing interest in Brittany and the South of France. This alone was a sign of great independance, since the provinces they chose,

Brittany and Provence, had attempted to preserve their customs, culture, and original language : indeed, on several occasions in history, these provinces had firmly opposed French nationalism. The artists concentrated on capturing the ephemeral in studies of the particular light and colors found in the different regions where they set up their easels. Then, settled in the provinces, they gradually abandoned observed reality in favor of a more intellectual kind of painting and devoted themselves to painting purely imaginary landscapes. Cézanne's art would soon lead to Cubism : the real landscape became a mere pretext for investigations that transcend it.

Already in 1907, Proust had eloquently analyzed the originality of Monet's universe : " ... if... one day I am able to visit Claude Monet's garden, I feel certain that what I shall see there, in a garden of tones and colors more than of flowers, will be less the customary floral garden than a color garden,... flowers arranged to form a pattern that is not quite nature's, since they have been planted in such a way that flowers of matching shades blossom together, harmonizing infinitely in an expanse of pink or blue, and which the painter's powerfully revealed intention has dematerialized, in a way, of all that is not color... " (" Les *Éblouissements*, par la comtesse de Noailles, " *Le Figaro*, June 15, 1907).

The walls of the Musée d'Orsay, located in the heart of Paris on the banks of the river the Impressionnists loved, are like an invitation for a day in the country. At the same time, the collections that have been brought together in the museum retrace the fascinating evolution — from figurative canvases to more abstract works — that led to " modern " landscape : the Musée d'Orsay can thus also be seen as the link between the Musée du Louvre and the Centre National d'Art et de Culture Georges Pompidou.

> " ... The Louvre is the book in which we learn to read. We must do more, however, than simply copy the beautiful expressions of our illustrious predecessors. We must venture into the out-of-doors to study the beauties of nature, and try to hear what nature is telling us. And we must strive to express ourselves guided by our own individual natures... "
> Cézanne, in a letter to Émile Bernard, 1905

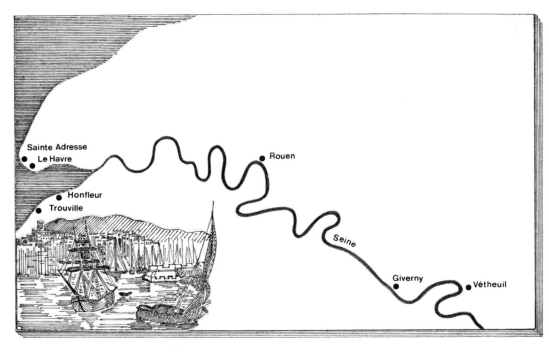

Sainte Adresse
Le Havre
Honfleur
Trouville
Rouen
Seine
Giverny
Vétheuil

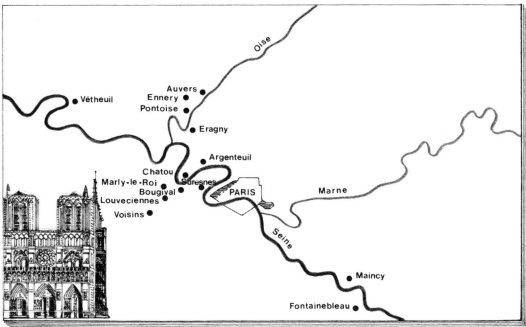

Oise
Vétheuil
Auvers
Ennery
Pontoise
Eragny
Argenteuil
Chatou
Marly-le-Roi
Bougival
Louveciennes
Voisins
Suresnes
PARIS
Marne
Seine
Maincy
Fontainebleau

Dressé par J. Coubariett.

14

# CHAPTER I : THE BARBIZON SCHOOL
# NATURALISTS AND REALISTS
# THE BEGINNINGS OF IMPRESSIONISM

*" Who are the painters I like ? To speak only of our contemporaries : Delacroix, Corot, Millet, Rousseau, and Courbet, our masters. All those who loved nature and could feel strongly... "*
Sisley to Adolphe Tavernier, January 1892

Readily recognizing their debt to the great names of the nineteenth-century French School, the Impressionists considered themselves the descendents of the Barbizon landscape painters. They followed in the steps of Théodore Rousseau, who spoke of his efforts to hear " the voice of the trees..., the language of the forests " (ill. 7). The Musée d'Orsay's Chauchard Collection, which contains major works by the greatest of the Barbizon artists (including, for instance, Millet's famous *Angelus*), is of enormous interest for the study of that school. The Impressionists' early works show the strong influence of Corot in particular : Berthe Morisot had, moreover, been his student. One of his canvases exhibited at the Salon of 1850-51, *A Morning, The Dance of the Nymphs* (ill. 11), illustrated the new orientation of Corot's art toward a highly personal vision of an imaginary world : this poetic, and quite Romantic, style, which could be seen as foreshadowing the Symbolist landscapes painted at the end of the century, was expressed in a vaporous, silvery tonality adopted several years later by the Impressionists.

The animals in the fields and forests particularly inspired Troyon, Daubigny, Rosa Bonheur (ill. 2, 8, 9), and Courbet, the master of Realism (ill. 3). On his return from hunting in Germany, Courbet sent a magnificent *Stag Fight* (ill. 10) to the Salon of 1861, noting : " the painting with three stags is an early spring landscape ; it shows the ground already covered in green, as the sap makes it way to the top of the tallest trees... "

Millet first chose naturalistic scenes of the peasants he had observed working in the fields around Barbizon and Chailly : among the works exhibited at the Salon of 1857 was *The Gleaners* (ill. 12). On May 30, 1863, Millet wrote to Sensier : " There are some who say I rob the country of its charms. But, I find something much greater than charm in the country : infinite splendors... I clearly see the aureoles around the dandelions, and the sun shining far off in the distance, beyond the countryside, its glorious rays illuminating the clouds... " This letter reveals the painter's growing interest in landscape which, no longer a background, was becoming the subject of the picture. Shortly before his death, the artist turned to the

Classical theme of the cycle of the seasons, which had also been treated, in a quite traditional way, by Daubigny (ill. 6, 9). But, Millet totally renewed the traditional approach to this theme : with the presence of the rainbow and the important role played by light, Millet's *Spring* (ill. 14), painted on the eve of the first Impressionist exhibition in 1874, foreshadowed the flowering orchards painted by Pissarro, Monet, and Sisley, who so loved to celebrate the arrival of spring.

In Manet's *Luncheon on the Grass* (ill. 15), which created a scandal at the Salon des Refusés in 1863, the surrounding landscape is still being used as a background for the figures. If it cannot but suggest the Italian masters (Raphael, Giorgione, Titian), the nude, represented in a scene from contemporary life, also evokes a " day in the country, " a highly " modern " subject. This historic work also shows the advent of a lightened palette.

The insertion of figures in the landscape was also the young Monet's goal in his large *Luncheon on the Grass,* painted for the Salon of 1866 (ill. 18). The canvas, painted from a preliminary sketch, was abandoned, then cut up into sections : the Musée d'Orsay possesses the left-side fragment. Bazille posed for several of the figures found in *Luncheon on the Grass ;* it is thus hardly surprising that Monet's artistic investigations influenced the early efforts of his friend from Gleyre's studio. The *Forest of Fontaine-bleau* (ill. 17) constitutes one of Bazille's last attempts to represent the Ile-de-France countryside. Like Monet, Bazille was then in search of a new direction.

On February 2, 1867, the painter Dubourg wrote to Boudin : "Monet... has a canvas that is nearly three meters high and proportionately long : the figures, a bit smaller than lifesize, are elegantly dressed women picking flowers in a garden ; the canvas was begun from nature, out-of-doors. " Dubourg was describing *Women in the Garden* (ill. 19). In this work, refused at the Salon of 1867, Monet succeeded in expressing the spontaneity of his vision ; observing the play of sunlight through the foliage, he reproduced the sharp contrast of light and shade on the ground. *Women in the Garden,* certainly influenced *Family Reunion,* and was accepted at the Salon of 1868.

" ...I've just spent a week in the little village of Chailly near the Forest of Fontainebleau. I was with my friend Monet... who has quite a flair for landscape. The advice he gave me has proved most helpful. "
Bazille, in a letter to his mother, 1863

1. Jules Dupré: *La Mare aux chênes*, 1850-1855. *Pond with Oak Trees.*

2. Rosa Bonheur:
*Labourage nivernais,*
1849.
*Plowing in the
Nivernais: The Dressing
of the Vines.*

3. Gustave Courbet:
*Remise de
chevreuils,* 1866.
*Gathering of Deer.*

4. Antoine Barye:
*Les Gorges
d'Apremont,
forêt
de Fontainebleau.*
s.d. *The Apremont
Gorges, Forest
of Fontainebleau.*

5. Léon Belly:
*Les Foins en
Normandie*, s.d.
*Hay in Normandy.*

6. Charles-François
Daubigny:
*La Moisson*, 1851.
*Harvest Time.*

7. Théodore Rousseau:
*Clairière dans la haute futaie,*
*forêt de Fontainebleau,*
dit *La Charrette*, 1862.
*Clearing in the Forest of*
*Fontainebleau,* known as *The Cart.*

9. Charles-François Daubigny:
*Les Vendanges en Bourgogne*, 1863.
*Harvesting the Grapes in Burgundy.*

10. Gustave Courbet:
*Le Combat de cerfs.*
*Le rut du printemps,*
1861.
*Stag Fight. The Spring Rut.*

11. Jean-Baptiste Camille
Corot: *Une matinée,
la danse des nymphes,*
1850-1851.
*A Morning, Dance of
the Nymphs.*

12. Jean-François Millet:
*Les Glaneuses,*
1857.
*The Gleaners.*

13. Bastien-Lepage:
*Les Foins*, 1877.
*Hay.*

14. Jean-François Millet:
*Le Printemps,*
1868-1873.
*Spring.*

29

15. Édouard Manet:
*Le Déjeuner sur l'herbe,*
1863.
*Luncheon on the Grass.*

16. Claude Monet: *Le Pavé de Chailly*, 1865. *Cobblestone Road, Chailly.*

17. Frédéric Bazille: *Forêt de Fontainebleau*, 1865. *Forest of Fontainebleau.*

18. Claude Monet:
Fragment du *Déjeuner
sur l'herbe*,
vers 1865-1866.
Section of *Luncheon on
the Grass.*

19. Claude Monet:
*Femmes au jardin,*
1867.
*Women in the Garden.*

33

## CHAPTER II : PONTOISE AND AUVERS-SUR-OISE

" Cézanne... was influenced by me at Pontoise, and I by him... What is curious in the Cézanne exhibition at Vollard's is the relation between certain of his Auvers and Pontoise landscapes and my own. Of course, we were always together back then ; but, one thing is certain, each of us kept the only thing that really matters, his ' sensation '. "

Pissarro, in a letter to his son Lucien, November 22, 1895

*P*issarro was referring to the experiences he had shared with Cézanne some twenty years earlier. If Bougival, Louveciennes, Marly-le-Roi, and Argenteuil gave the Impressionists the opportunity to paint the " modern suburbs, " the region around Pontoise and Auvers-sur-Oise, on the other hand, favored rural landscape painting and the representation of traditional villages. Monet moved to Argenteuil in 1871 (see Chapter IV) ; the following year, Pissarro settled in Pontoise, where he originated the naturalistic current, based on rural themes, that he introduced in Impressionism : a group, which included Cézanne, Gauguin, and Guillaumin, formed around the " father " of the Impressionists.

" In front of his easel, his colors carefully classed on his palette as he worked to spread the clear sky over the entire landscape, Pissarro forgot about everything that was not a part of the scene he had chosen, which always corresponded to his deepest feelings. He was a country fellow who loved his village, its gardens, the fields adjoining the rustic houses, the bubbling streams and winding rivers down in the valley, the paths lined with flowering hedges, the orchards of apple trees adorned with graceful pink and white blossoms, and the red and golden harvests, " Gustave Geffroy wrote in 1922.

The titles of Pissarro's works reveal the artist's familiarity with the region around Pontoise : after working at the Côte des Grouettes and the Hermitage in 1873-74 (ill. 22), he turned his attention to the red tile roofs of the houses at the foot of the Côte des Bœufs in 1877. The construction of the resulting composition *(Red Roofs, Corner of a Village in Winter* (ill. 25) reveals the influence Cézanne exerted on his elder. Conversely, certain of Cézanne's canvases show the influence of Pissarro ; however, as Pissarro himself insisted in his 1895 letter to his son, each artist kept his own distinct personality.

Indeed, if both artists liked to represent rural areas and villages that had not been altered by modernization (with the exception of the railroad), there are major differences in their treatment of landscape ; and, these differences can largely be explained in terms of the artists' different temperaments. Thus, Pissarro animated fields and villages with peasants and animals (the horse-drawn cart in *Ennery Road near Pontoise* is a characteristic example of this, and a traditional motif in the artist's works ; ill. 24), whereas the places Cézanne painted are completely deserted (ill. 20, 21, 28). Pissarro's inhabited landscapes can be opposed to the pure landscapes analyzed by Cézanne. Moreover, Pissarro tended to represent panoramic views (e.g., the marvellous view in the previously mentioned *Ennery Road near Pontoise*) and label these views with titles specifying their location, whereas Cézanne was more interested in isolated motifs — whether a house (ill. 20, 21), trees, or a bridge (ill. 28) — than in general topographical study.

At the first Impressionist exhibition in 1874, Pissarro displayed his *Hoarfrost* (ill. 23), a painting which provoked a bitingly ironic reaction from the critic Louis Leroy, usually remembered today for his early use of the term "Impressionism," who wrote in *Le Charivari :* " Is that supposed to be a frost-covered field ?... It's nothing but palette scapings spread over a dirty canvas. Just try to figure it out ! It's impossible to tell the top from the bottom, or the front from the back... " The exhibition also included Cézanne's *House of the Hanged Man* (ill. 20), painted by the artist while he was staying at Doctor Gachet's in Auvers-sur-Oise : influenced by Pissarro, he had lightened his palette and adopted the division-of-tones technique used by the Impressionists ; he did, however, continue to use a thick impasto ; and, of course, his primary concern was still construction. The work was badly greeted by the critics.

" ...as for landscape, M. Cézanne will be pleased to learn that we will not be discussing his *House of the Hanged Man*... as a matter of fact, we are still trying to figure it out. "
Marc de Montifaud, *L'Artiste,* May 1, 1874

20. Paul Cézanne:
*La Maison du pendu,*
1873.
*The House of the
Hanged Man.*

21. Paul Cézanne:
*La Maison du docteur
Gachet à Auvers,*
vers 1873.
*Doctor Gachet's House
in Auvers.*

22. Camille Pissarro:
*Coteau de l'Hermitage,
Pontoise*, 1873.
*Hillside in the
Hermitage, Pontoise.*

23. Camille Pissarro:
*Gelée blanche*, 1873.
*Hoarfrost.*

24. Camille Pissarro:
*Route d'Ennery près
Pontoise,* 1874.
The Ennery Road
near Pontoise.

25. Camille Pissarro:
*Les Toits rouges, coin
de village, effet d'hiver,*
1877.
*Red Roofs, a Corner of
the Village in Winter.*

26. Camille Pissarro:
*Potager et arbres
en fleurs,
printemps,
Pontoise*, 1877.
*Kitchen Garden and
Flowering Trees,
Spring, Pontoise.*

27. Camille Pissarro:
*La Brouette, verger*,
vers 1881.
*The Wheelbarrow
(Orchard).*

28. Paul Cézanne:
*Le Pont de Maincy,*
1879-1880.
*The Maincy Bridge.*

29. Armand Guillaumin:
*Paysage de plaine,*
vers 1878.
*Landscape. A Plain.*

# CHAPTER III : BOUGIVAL, CHATOU, LOUVECIENNES, AND MARLY-LE-ROI

" ...Would you like to see the richest and most picturesque region around Paris, one that has been so rightly praised ?... If so, set out early in the morning for Bougival ; and, after a big lunch on the banks of the river, proceed to Marly-le-Roi on the path that goes through Louveciennes... it's the path the schoolboys use... "

Victorien Sardou, *Paris-Guide par les principaux écrivains et artistes de la France,* 1867 (published for the Exposition Universelle in Paris).

*W*hen the future Impressionists decided to break with their elders by abandoning the Forest of Fontainebleau, Sisley, Monet, Renoir, and Pissarro chose to paint (in what was already a quite recognizable style) this region outside of Paris. Doubtless, the rapid transport link to the capital played a part in their choosing this particular part of Ile-de-France, already on its way to becoming a suburb of Paris ; however, somewhat earlier, the poet Gérard de Nerval had extolled the area's country charm (*Promenades et souvenirs,* 1855). This region can truly be considered the " cradle of Impressionism. "

Between Bougival and Chatou, on the little island of Croissy, the *Grenouillère* was a popular destination for Parisians out for a day in the country : it was a sort of open-air café where customers could dance, drink, and swim. During the summer of 1869, Monet and Renoir worked there together. Their respective approaches to landscape proved to be very different from the start, Renoir already showing the particular interest in figures that later guided his work at Chatou and Bougival (ill. 45, 47), whereas Monet devoted most of his time to studying the landscape and the light reflecting on the water. If the investigations that Monet and Renoir carried out at *La Grenouillère* are always discussed by historians of Impressionism, Monet's experience working side-by-side with Pissarro at Louveciennes the following year, on the other hand, often goes unmentioned. Although he continued to paint traditional country landscapes, Pissarro did feel the effect of Monet's influence. He often represented *The Versailles Road* (ill. 32, 33, 35) that went by his house in Louveciennes, a subject also treated by Monet.

Sisley, who often set up his easel in Bougival between 1872 and 1877, had settled in Voisins-Louveciennes in 1871, not far from the parents of another painter, Renoir, who often visited and worked with him. In 1872, Pissarro represented the *Entrance to the Village of Voisins* (inserted in the May triptych ; ill. 30) ; Sisley too painted several views of this little village (ill. 31), emphasizing the friendliness of the landscape with human figures. Although he never obtained the nationality of his country of adoption, this artist, British by birth, was marvellously successful in rendering the luminosity of the Ile-de-France countryside, of which he here gives a serene vision.

Of all the Impressionists, Sisley stayed on the longest in this region. From 1874 to 1877, he resided in Marly-le-Roi. He was particularly drawn to the park in Marly, as his magnificent *Watering Place at Marly* shows. Louveciennes and Marly inspired him to do many winter landscapes : these paintings, which show the artist's sensitivity to the silent mystery of the snowy countryside, corresponded perfectly to his reserved and solitary character (they are also, it should be noted, closely related to the winter landscapes that Monet and Pissarro had done earlier ; ill. 40-42). Sisley's search for clearness and sense of construction, probably inherited from Corot, led him to continue using terraced planes. Indeed, the road disappearing in the horizon was one of his favorite themes : the painter remembered Hobbema's famous *Middleharnis Path* (London, The National Gallery) for the daring composition of *The Road, View of Sèvres Path, Louveciennes,* which has recently been identified as the path that goes by the *machine de Marly* (ill. 34). The transportation system (roads, bridges, trains...) was an integral part of the rapidly evolving " modern landscape " (ill. 43, 44).

In 1880, Renoir went to Chatou, staying at the Fournaise restaurant on an island in the Seine ; the previous year, he had painted the owner's wife in a canvas that was formerly known as *At La Grenouillère* (ill. 45) ; he then undertook his major *Oarsmen's Lunch* (Washington, The Phillips Collection). During 1882-83, drawing his inspiration from the leisure activities of town and country, he executed three works based on a dancing couple : the pair exhibited at the Musée d'Orsay (*City Dance* and *Country Dance,* ill. 47) was once seen, in 1886, as expressing an opposition between the seasons of winter and summer.

Finally, Berthe Morisot spent several summers at Bougival and recorded her stays in sun-drenched, sparklingly gay canvases : often depicting her husband Eugène Manet, the painter's brother, and their daughter Julie, or else her sister Edma (ill. 46), these canvases show the artist's mastery of plein-air painting and the insertion of the human figure in the landscape.

" ...Mademoiselle Berthe Morisot takes us into damp and dewy meadows... she likes the tall grass where a young woman can sit down, book in hand, with a child. She confronts the charming artifice of the Parisian woman with the charm of nature... "
Jean Prouvaire, " L'Exposition du boulevard des Capucines ", *Le Rappel,* April 20, 1874

30. Camille Pissarro:
*Entrée du village
de Voisins*, 1872.
*Entrance of the Village of Voisins.*

31. Alfred Sisley:
*Village de Voisins,*
1874.
*Village of Voisins.*

49

32. Camille Pissarro:
*La Diligence à
Louveciennes,*
1870. *Coach
at Louveciennes.*

33. Camille Pissarro:
*La Route de*
*Louveciennes*, 1870.
*Road at Louveciennes.*

34. Alfred Sisley:
*La Route,
vue du chemin de
Sèvres,* dit aussi
*le Chemin
de la Machine,
Louveciennes,* 1873.
*The Road, View of
Sèvres Path,*
also known
as
*The Machine Path,
Louveciennes.*

35. Camille Pissarro:
*La Route de
Louveciennes,* 1872.
*Road at
Louveciennes.*

36. Camille Pissarro:
*Châtaigniers à
Louveciennes,*
vers 1872.
*Chestnut Trees at
Louveciennes.*

55

37. Camille Pissarro:
*Paysage d'hiver à*
*Louveciennes,*
vers 1870.
*Winter Landscape,*
*Louveciennes.*

38. Alfred Sisley:
*Louveciennes, hauteurs
de Marly*, vers 1873.
*Louveciennes. The
Heights of Marly.*

39. Berthe Morisot:
*Dans les blés*, 1875.
*In the Wheat.*

40. Alfred Sisley:
*La Neige à*
*Marly-le-Roi*, 1875.
*Snow*
*at Marly-le-Roi.*

41. Alfred Sisley:
*Route de*
*Louveciennes*
*sous la neige,*
vers 1877-1878.
*Road*
*at Louveciennes*
*in the Snow.*

42. Alfred Sisley: *La Neige à Louveciennes*, 1878.
*Snow at Louveciennes.*

43. Claude Monet:
*Train dans la campagne,*
vers 1870-1871.
*Train in the Countryside.*

44. Pierre-Auguste
Renoir: *Pont du chemin
de fer à Chatou*, 1881.
*Railway Bridge at
Chatou.*

45. Pierre Auguste
Renoir: *Alfonsine
Fournaise*, 1879.

46. Berthe Morisot:
*La Chasse aux
papillons*, 1874.
*Butterfly Hunting.*

47. Pierre-Auguste
Renoir: *Danse à la
campagne,*
1882-1883.
*Country Dance.*

## CHAPTER IV : ARGENTEUIL

" Arriving at the Neuilly Bridge, M. Dufour had exclaimed : ' Here we are in the country at last ! '...

" At the square in Courbevoie, they had been overcome with wonder at the distance of the horizon. To the right, down below, was Argenteuil, its steeple silhouetted against the sky ; higher up, were the hills around Sannois... "

Maupassant, *Une partie de campagne,* 1881

*D*uring the 1870s, Impressionism flourished in Argenteuil, the town that could be said to symbolize the movement's " heroic " period. Shortly after he arrived in Argenteuil, Monet wrote to Pissarro on December 21, 1871 : "...we're still caught up in the confusion of moving in. " This was the artist's first house in Argenteuil ; apparently, he had found it through Manet. Monet invited Sisley and Renoir to Argenteuil, and spent time with them there on his return from England. In a letter dated January 2, 1872, Boudin wrote : " We often see Monet, for whom we had a house-warming just the other day ; his new home is quite nice, and he really seems to want to make a name for himself... I believe he is destined to become one of the leading figures in our school. " Thanks to sales to the Impressionists' friend and dealer Durand-Ruel, 1872-1873 were relatively prosperous years for Monet. This temporary comfort is reflected in the artist's work from the period. The different views of the house and luxuriant garden in Argenteuil suggest a most agreeable life. The artist was able to study the splendors of spring in his own garden ; he captured the instantaneity of his vision of lilacs in bloom in two canvases that form a pair : *Lilacs, Grey Weather* (ill. 49) and *Lilacs in the Sun* (Moscow, Pushkin Museum of Fine Arts). Foreshadowing his later interest in the " series, " he here treated the same motif under changing atmospheric conditions. The figures shaded by the trees, which seem to blend into the vegetation, have been identified as the painter's wife Camille and, possibly, Sisley accompanied by his wife (yet another reminder of Sisley's trips over to Argenteuil when he was living in Voisins-Louveciennes). Like Monet, Sisley represented the little square in Argenteuil, the sun shining on a row of houses that contrast with those left in the shade (ill. 54).

It is the back of Monet's first house at Argenteuil that forms the background of the composition entitled *The Luncheon* (ill. 50). The artist's son Jean (born in 1867) is seen absorbed in play next to the table, shown after the meal has been finished. A certain image of the art of country living is given here : each detail, though apparently anecdotal at first glance, contributes to the creation of a feeling of comfort and prosperity : the profusion of flowers, the elegance of the dresses and whiteness of the linen, the arrangement of the dishes and, in particular, the bowl of fruit, the table settings and fine china... Using the gardens of the two houses he occupied successively in Argenteuil, the painter described more an urban than a rural universe : in their gardens near the capital, leisure-seeking Parisians had, it should be remembered, recreated a disciplined landscape in keeping with their urban vision. In *The Luncheon,* the foliage and flowers, as well as the alliance of greens and reds, recall the painter's *Flowering Garden* (ill. 56). The division of highly contrasting areas of light and shade plays an important role here as well, as does the insertion of figures in the landscape. In this work, displayed at the second Impressionist exhibition in 1876 under the designation of " decorative panel, " Monet returned to the large format he had used in his early works (ill. 18, 19). The decorative and intimist character of this scene, like its composition and the terraced planes, foreshadows Bonnard's charming compositions (ill. 79).

Monet also took advantage of the countryside around Argenteuil : that he could be captivated by a more rural landscape is seen in the quivering grass of the famous field of *Poppies* (ill. 51), a canvas he presented at the first Impressionist exhibition in 1874. As elsewhere, the painter played on the effects produced by juxtaposing complementary colors, the reds literally bursting out of the greens, whence the extraordinary luminosity of the canvas. Painted in the same gay spirit as *Flowering Garden,* this colorful, sun-drenched field, seen at a certain distance, is quite characteristic of Monet's style during the period that Impressionism flourished. Many years later at Giverny (ill. 78), the artist returned to the beloved subject of a profusely flowering garden ; the young woman with a parasol and the child are probably Camille and Jean Monet. Renoir shared Monet's feelings for Argenteuil ; and, his *Uphill Path in Tall Grass* (ill. 52) is similar in spirit to *Poppies.* The two painters often worked together on the banks of the Argenteuil Basin, painting the leisure activities of sailing, rowing, and simple strolls (ill. 53). As shown in the images the Impressionists and their friend Caillebotte have left us of it, Argenteuil was a pleasant resort for the Parisian bourgeoisie, a combination of town and country in the process of becoming a " modern suburb. " This duality is illustrated by Monet's panoramic view of the area from the heights of Sannois (ill. 48).

" At first glance, it is hard to see what differentiates M. Monet's paintings from M. Sisley's, and the latter's from M. Pissarro's. A little study will quickly reveal that M. Monet is the most daring, M. Sisley the most harmonious and the most timorous, M. Pissarro the most realistic and the most naive. "
Armand Silvestre, 1873

48. Claude Monet:
*Paysage:*
*vue de plaine à*
*Argenteuil,* 1872.
*Landscape:*
*The Plain at*
*Argenteuil.*

49. Claude Monet:
*Le Repos sous les lilas,*
vers 1873.
*Resting under the Lilacs.*

50. Claude Monet:
*Le Déjeuner*, vers 1873.
*The Luncheon.*

51. Claude Monet:
*Coquelicots,* 1873.
*Poppies.*

52. Pierre-Auguste Renoir: *Chemin montant dans les hautes herbes,* vers 1876-1878. *Uphill Path in Tall Grass.*

53. Claude Monet:
*Le Bassin d'Argenteuil,*
1875.
*The Argenteuil Basin.*

54. Alfred Sisley: *Place à Argenteuil*, 1872.
*A Square in Argenteuil.*

## CHAPTER V : TRAVELS IN NORMANDY AND BRITTANY

*" As soon as we arrived in Honfleur, we found our landscape motifs. They were easy to find, for this is a paradise... "*
Bazille, in a letter to his mother, August, 1864

*T*he future Impressionists shared the Barbizon painters' feelings for Normandy. As early as 1864, Monet, accompanied by Bazille, had painted works there which show the influence of Troyon and Daubigny. In the letter quoted above, Bazille added : " We eat at the Saint-Siméon farm located on the cliff a little above Honfleur. That's where we spend our days working " : the whitened roof of the building is seen on the left of the *Snow-Covered Road* Monet painted somewhat later (ill. 58). The place thus became a meeting point for the new generation as, along with the villages of Barbizon and Chailly-en-Bière, it had been for their predecessors.

Much more modest in format than *Women in the Garden* (ill. 19), this canvas (ill. 56) does, however, also bear the mark of the artist's plein-air investigations in 1866-67. As in other works from this period, the canvas is divided into zones of light and shade : by leaving the left-hand portion of the foreground in the shade, the artist was able to heighten the intensity of the light provided by the blue summer sky. A major concern of Monet's was to capture the spontaneity of his first sun-drenched impression, expressed here by means of color contrasts : the red notes provided by the geraniums and roses burst forth from the green vegetation, sparkling in the light, like the *Poppies* scattered through the fields around Argenteuil (ill. 51). This particular treatment of flowerbeds in bloom is seen from the beginning of the artist's career : as in *Women in the Garden,* we are shown a typical garden of the period in which the clumps of roses play an important decorative role. It should be noted that Monet was already painting in fragmented strokes, the technique that would soon epitomize Impressionism.

Following the example of Courbet's winter landscapes, Monet was drawn to the snow theme early on and treated it in a spectacular way during his 1868-69 visit to Étretat, the beloved land of Maupassant. In December, 1868, Monet wrote to Bazille : " ...I often go out in the country that is so lovely here, and I think it may even be nicer in winter than summer ; naturally, I work all the time, wherever I go ; and, I do believe I am going to do some serious things this year. " The exceptionally large size of the winter landscape in which *The Magpie* looks so alone (ill. 57) and the fact that this masterpiece seems to be the result of a challenge the painter had set himself, i.e., to express light and density by playing on the range of different whites, were enough to ensure, as might have been guessed, that this would be one of the two Monet pictures refused by the jury of the Salon of 1868.

In 1864, Pissarro left the Pontoise region to settle permanently in Éragny-sur-Epte, near Gisors. There, he studied the countryside around Éragny, the peasants, and the market at Gisors ; and, his brush sometimes transformed these subjects into a quite original vision : indeed, it was at this time that Pissarro made several attempts at Pointillism, such as his picture of the *Woman in the Field* (ill. 62), and even presented several works in this new style next to those of Seurat and Signac at the eighth Impressionist exhibition in 1886. At the third Impressionist exhibition in 1877, Pissarro had shown a canvas painted the previous summer in Mayenne : *Harvest at Montfoucault* (ill. 63). The grainstacks theme found in this picture would later be made famous by Monet.

Monet never budged from the right bank of the Seine, but did move farther and farther away from the capital : after Argenteuil, he went to Vétheuil (ill. 59) and, finally, in 1883, settled in Giverny, southwest of Vernon, in Eure, between Ile-de-France and Normandy. On October 7, 1890, Monet wrote to Gustave Geffroy : "...I am set on doing a series showing the effects of changing light (grainstacks)... the more I advance, the more I realize how much work it will take to achieve what I'm after : 'instantaneity,' the envelope created by the same light spread everywhere..." That year, the artist passionately devoted himself to representing the *Grainstacks* at Giverny. In the more than twenty versions that make up this first real "series", Monet captured the ephemerality of morning, afternoon, and evening light as it varied not only with the time of day, but also with the changing seasons, from late summer (when the Musée d'Orsay canvas was painted ; ill. 65) into autumn and winter (with snow, fog, frost, and thawing.

Gauguin also represented the harvest in Brittany during his stays there in 1888 and 1889 (ill. 64, 66). During the summer of 1888, Sérusier (see Chapter VI), Gauguin and Bernard worked in the Bois-d'Amour near Pont-Aven ; it was there that Bernard painted the monumental landscape with his young sister Madeleine (ill. 68).

" I love Brittany. I find wildness and primitiveness there. When my clogs echo on the granite beneath them, I hear the muted, dull and powerful tone I am trying to achieve in my paintings. "
Gauguin, in a letter to Schuffenecker, February, 1888

55. Claude Monet:
*Cour de ferme*
*en Normandie,*
vers 1864.
*A Barnyard in*
*Normandy.*

56. Claude Monet:
*Jardin en fleurs*,
vers 1866.
*Flowering Garden.*

57. Claude Monet:
*La Pie*, 1868-1869.
*The Magpie.*

58. Claude Monet:
*La Charrette. Route sous
la neige à Honfleur,*
vers 1867.
*The Cart. Snow-Covered
Road at Honfleur.*

60. Camille Pissarro:
*Effet de neige à Éragny,*
1894.
*Snow at Éragny.*

61. Camille Pissarro:
*Paysage à Éragny
(église et ferme
d'Éragny),* 1895.
*Landscape:
Church and
Farm at Éragny.*

62. Camille Pissarro:
*Femme dans un
clos, soleil de
printemps dans
le pré à Éragny,*
1887.
*Woman in a Field,
Spring Sun, Éragny.*

63. Camille Pissarro:
*La Moisson à
Montfoucault*, 1876.
*Harvest Time at
Montfoucault.*

64. Paul Gauguin:
*La Fenaison en
Bretagne*, 1888.
*Haymaking Time in
Brittany.*

65. Claude Monet:
*Meules, fin de l'été,
effet du matin,* 1890.
*Grainstacks, End of
Summer, Morning.*

66. Paul Gauguin:
*Les Meules jaunes,*
1889.
*Golden Grainstacks.*

67. Paul Sérusier: *La Barrière fleurie*, 1889. *Fence in Bloom.*

68. Émile Bernard:
*Madeleine au Bois
d'Amour*, 1888.
*Madeleine in the Bois
d'Amour.*

69. Paul Gauguin:
*Paysage de Bretagne.*
*Le moulin David*, 1894.
*Brittany Landscape,*
*David Mill.*

# CHAPTER VI: INTO THE TWENTIETH CENTURY

> " The spectacle created by the sky, water, and verdure varies with every passing moment, the first Impressionists told us... Hence the necessity of capturing a landscape in one sitting, hence an inclination to make nature grimace in order to prove conclusively that each and every moment is unique... The neo-Impressionists endeavor to synthesize a landscape so as to preserve the sensation implicit in it. Moreover, their approach rules out all haste and necessitates work in the studio... "
>
> Félix Fénéon, " Le néo-impressionisme, " *L'Art moderne,* May 1, 1887

*F*rom 1860 to 1880, the Impressionists' preferred spots had been either in and around Paris or on the Normandy coast. As travel and tourism developed, the aging Impressionists, along with the younger neo-Impressionists, moved farther and farther away from the capital to venture into largely unexplored regions such as Brittany and the South of France.

As we consider Sérusier's *The Talisman,* painted at Pont-Aven (ill. 70), it might be helpful to recall the testimony of Maurice Denis: " It was in the early fall of 1888 that we first heard Gauguin's name mentioned, when Sérusier came back from Pont-Aven and showed us, rather mysteriously, a cigar box lid on which an odd-looking landscape had been painted: it was odd because it was so synthetically formulated, painted in violet, scarlet, Veronese green, and other pure colors right out of the tube, with no admixture of white. ' How does that tree look to you ? ' Gauguin had asked in a corner of the Bois-d'Amour. ' Is it really green ? Then use green, the most beautiful green on your palette. And does that shadow look rather blue ? Then don't be afraid to paint it as blue as possible ' " (" L'influence de Paul Gauguin, " *L'Occident,* October, 1903). Sérusier's small, historic landscape, which so strongly exemplifies Gauguin's daring lesson, was considered a *Talisman* by the Nabis ; they saw it as the origin of a new kind of painting, which Maurice Denis succinctly defined in the following terms : " A painting, before being a battle horse, a nude woman, or some kind of anecdote, is essentially a surface plane covered with colors applied in a certain pattern " (Manifesto of the Nabi Movement in *Art et Critique,* August, 1890). The subject was being eliminated from painting to leave the dominant place, henceforth, to color.

Also in October, 1888, Gauguin accepted Van Gogh's invitation and went to Arles. Van Gogh thus came under the influence of the School of Pont-Aven, but also influenced Gauguin, whom he encouraged to read Loti. Van Gogh's dream of founding a " Studio of the South " became, for Gauguin, the dream of a " Studio of the Tropics." Van Gogh helped Gauguin decide on his great departure for Tahiti, which was to lead to a Symbolist and richly exotic art. In Arles, Gauguin put his advice to Sérusier into practice ; *The Roman Burial Ground at Arles* (ill. 71), with the orange-red spot in the foreground, foreshadows the Fauves' bold use of color (Vlaminck, ill. 74), as do the canvases Van Gogh painted during the last two months of his life (1890) in Auvers-sur-Oise (ill. 72, 73). "...I am out in the characteristic and picturesque heart of the country," the artist wrote at that time ; speaking of *The Church at Auvers-sur-Oise,* he added, " the color is probably more expressive and sumptuous." These landscapes by Van Gogh cleared the way for twentieth-century movements such as Fauvism and Expressionism.

Returning to his birthplace, Aix-en-Provence, Cézanne gave an utterly personal interpretation of the Provençal landscape ; he often worked out-of-.doors in the Parc de Château-Noir (ill. 75). Outlined against the Midi sky, as if cut out by the light itself, Sainte-Victoire mountain became the painter's preferred motif. In 1907, the fifth Salon d'Automne devoted a posthumous retrospective to the master from Aix, only a year after his death. Cézanne's powerful influence on a new generation had already begun : twentieth-century artists have never stopped studying the works of Cézanne (Matisse owned the landscape mentioned above ; ill. 75), who could be said to have opened the road to Cubism and abstraction. " I believe the young painters are more intelligent than the others... " was Cézanne's presentiment when he wrote to his son several days before his death (letter dated October 15, 1906).

By the end of the century, the Midi had become one of the painters' favorite regions. Putting the new theories of Divisionism into practice, the neo-Impressionists (Seurat, Signac, Cross) tried to capture the Mediterranean light (ill. 77). Even Pissarro, for a time, adopted the Pointillist technique (ill. 60, 62).

Like Cézanne, Monet chose a certain isolation : "I am in ecstasy ; Giverny is a splendid place for me," the artist wrote the critic Duret on May 20, 1883. He lived to a very old age, for his death came well into the twentieth century, in 1926. As the seasons came and went, Monet never stopped painting the flowers in his garden ; and, the description of Giverny given by Octave Mirbeau perfectly fits the canvas in the Musée d'Orsay (ill. 78) : " ...a house roughcast in pink mortar at the far end of the garden, always dazzling with flowers. It is spring... in the broad flowerbeds they border, against a background of blossoming orchards, the iris lift their strange, flouncy

*(Continued on page 110)*

70. Paul Sérusier:
*Le Talisman*, 1888.
*The Talisman.*

71. Paul Gauguin:
*Les Alyscamps,*
1888.
*The Roman Burial
Ground at Arles.*

72. Vincent van Gogh:
*L'Église d'Auvers,* 1890.
*Church in Auvers.*

73. Vincent van Gogh:
*Le Jardin du docteur
Gachet*, 1890.
*Doctor Gachet's Garden.*

74. Maurice de
Vlaminck: *Restaurant à
Marly-le-Roi*, vers 1905.
*Restaurant at
Marly-le-Roi.*

75. Paul Cézanne:
*Rochers près des grottes*
*au-dessus de*
*Château-Noir, vers 1904.*
*Rocks near the Caves*
*above Château-Noir.*

76. Georges Seurat:
*Lisière de bois au
printemps,* vers 1882.
*Edge of the Woods in
Spring.*

77. Henri-Edmond
Cross: *Les Cyprès
à Cagnes,* 1908.
*Cypress Trees at
Cagnes.*

78. Claude Monet:
*Le Jardin de Monet à
Giverny,* 1900.
*Monet's Garden at
Giverny.*

79. Pierre Bonnard:
*Le Grand Jardin*, 1898.
*The Big Garden.*

80. Gustav Klimt:
*Rosiers sous les arbres,*
vers 1905.
*Rosebushes under Trees.*

(Continued from page 99)

petals trimmed in white, mauve, lilac, yellow, and blue..., their elaborate undersides conjuring up mysterious analogies and the kind of perverse, seductive dreams that orchids also arouse..." (*L'Art dans les deux Mondes,* March 7, 1891).

Monet's house seems to disappear behind the trees to make room for this profusion of flowers ; the sky is absent, as in a nearly contemporaneous work of Klimt's (ill. 80). Monet too would be recognized as one of the forerunners of abstract art.

The Nabis often emphasized the decorative character of gardens (ill. 79). As the century drew to a close, an osmosis of painting, sculpture, and the decorative arts took place ; and, this phenomenon is quite perceptible in the Musée d'Orsay's collections. Out of the explosion of trends and investigations which characterized this period, the rich diversity of artistic expression in the twentieth century was born.

" You see, a new artistic era is in the making... "
Cézanne, in a letter to Ch. Camoin, January 28, 1902

# ILLUSTRATIONS

**1.** Jules Dupré (1811-1889): *Pond with Oak Trees,* 1850-1855.
Canvas, 1.02 × 0.84. Bequest of A. Chauchard, 1909.
**2.** Rosa Bonheur (1822-1899): *Plowing in the Nivernais : The Dressing of the Vines,* 1849.
Canvas, 1.34 × 2.60. Allocated to the Musées nationaux, 1874.
**3.** Gustave Courbet (1819-1877): *Gathering of Deer,* 1866.
Canvas, 1.74 × 2.09. Gift of a group of art lovers, 1890.
**4.** Antoine Barye (1795-1875): *The Apremont Gorges, Forest of Fontainebleau,* n.d.
Canvas, 0.17 × 0.30. Gift of J. Zoubaloff, 1914 ; on permanent loan from the Louvre.
**5.** Léon Belly (1827-1877): *Hay in Normandy,* n.d.
Canvas, 0.71 × 0.93. Gift of Mme Urbain Belly, 1925.
**6.** Charles-François Daubigny (1817-1878): *Harvest Time,* 1851.
Canvas, 1.35 × 1.96. Purchased in 1853.
**7.** Théodore Rousseau (1812-1867): *Clearing in the Forest of Fontainebleau,* know as *The Cart.* c. 1863.
Wood, 0.28 × 0.53. Bequest of A. Chauchard, 1909.
**8.** Constant Troyon (1810-1865): *View from the Heights of Suresnes,* 1856.
Canvas, 0.97 × 1.39. Purchased by the State in 1862.
**9.** Charles-François Daubigny (1817-1878): *Harvesting the Grapes in Burgundy,* 1863.
Canvas, 1.72 × 2.94. Purchased in 1878.
**10.** Gustave Courbet: *Star Fight. The Spring Rut,* 1861.
Canvas, 3.55 × 5.07. Purchased in 1881.
**11.** Jean-Baptiste Camille Corot (1796-1875): *A Morning, Dance of the Nymphs,* 1850-1851.
Canvas, 0.98 × 1.31. Purchased in 1854 ; on permanent loan from the Louvre.

**12.** Jean-François Millet (1814-1875): *The Gleaners,* 1857.
Canvas, 0.83 × 1.11. Gift of Mme Pommery, 1887.
**13.** Jules Bastien-Lepage (1848-1884): *Hay,* 1877.
Canvas, 1.80 × 1.95. Purchased by the State in 1885.
**14.** Jean-François Millet : *Spring,* 1868-1873.
Canvas, 0.86 × 1.11. Gift of Mrs F. Hartmann, 1887.
**15.** Edouard Manet (1832-1883): *The Luncheon on the Grass,* 1863.
Canvas, 1.08 × 2.64. Gift of E. Moreau-Nélaton, 1906.
**16.** Claude Monet (1840-1926): *Cobblestone Road, Chailly,* 1865.
Canvas, 0.43 × 0.59. Gift of E. Moreau-Nélaton, 1906.
**17.** Frédéric Bazille (1841-1870): *The Forest of Fontainebleau,* 1865.
Canvas, 0.60 × 0.73. Gift of Mme Fantin-Latour, 1905.
**18.** Claude Monet: *Section of Luncheon on the Grass,* c. 1865-1866.
Canvas, 4.18 × 1.50. Gift of G. Wildenstein, 1957.
**19.** Claude Monet: *Women in the Garden,* 1867.
Canvas, 2.55 × 2.05. Purchased in 1921.
**20.** Paul Cézanne (1839-1906): *The House of the Hanged Man,* 1873.
Canvas, 0.55 × 0.66. Bequest of I. de Camondo, 1911.
**21.** Paul Cézanne: *Doctor Gachet's House, in Auvers,* c. 1873.
Canvas, 0.46 × 0.38. Gift of P. Gachet, 1951.
**22.** Camille Pissarro (1830-1903): *Hillside in the Hermitage, Pontoise,* 1873.
Canvas, 0.61 × 0.73. Acquired in payment of inheritance taxes, 1983.
**23.** Camille Pissarro: *Hoarfrost,* 1873.
Canvas, 0.65 × 0.93. Bequest of E. Mollard, 1972.
**24.** Camille Pissaro: *The Ennery Road, near Pontoise,* 1874.
Canvas, 0.55 × 0.92. Gift of M. and R. Kaganovitch, 1973.
**25.** Camille Pissaro: *Red Roofs, a Corner of the Village in Winter,* 1877.
Canvas, 0.54 × 0.65. Bequest of G. Caillebotte, 1894.

**26.** Camille Pissarro: *Kitchen Garden and Flowering trees, Spring, Pontoise,* 1877.
Canvas, 0.65 × 0.81. Bequest of G. Caillebotte, 1894.
**27.** Camille Pissaro: *The Wheelbarrow (Orchard),* c. 1881.
Canvas, 0.54 × 0.65. Bequest of G. Caillebotte, 1894.
**28.** Paul Cézanne: *The Maincy Bridge,* 1879-1880.
Canvas, 0.58 × 0.72. Purchased with funds from an anonymous Canadian donation, 1955.
**29.** Armand Guillaumin (1841-1927): *Landscape. A Plain,* c. 1878.
Canvas, 0.54 × 0.65. Bequest of A. Personnaz, 1937.
**30.** Camille Pissarro: *Entrance to the Village of Voisins,* 1872.
Canvas, 0.46 × 0.55. Gift of E. May, 1923.
**31.** Alfred Sisley (1839-1899): *The Village of Voisins,* 1874.
Canvas, 0.38 × 0.46. Bequest of I. de Camondo, 1911.
**32.** Camille Pissarro: *Coach at Louveciennes,* 1870.
Canvas, 0.25 × 0.35. Gift of E. Moreau-Nélaton, 1906.
**33.** Camille Pissarro: *Road at Louveciennes,* 1870.
Canvas, 0.46 × 0.55. Bequest of A. Personnaz, 1937.
**34.** Alfred Sisley: *The Road, View of Sèvres Path, Louveciennes,* also known as *The Machine Path,* 1873.
Canvas, 0.54 × 0.73. Gift of Joanny Peytel, 1914.
**35.** Camille Pissarro: *Road at Louveciennes,* 1872.
Canvas, 0.60 × 0.73. Gift of P. Gachet, 1951.
**36.** Camille Pissarro: *Chestnut Trees at Louveciennes,* c. 1872.
Canvas, 0.41 × 0.54. Gift of P. Gachet, 1954.
**37.** Camille Pissarro: *Winter Landscape, Louveciennes,* c. 1870.
Canvas, 0.37 × 0.46. Bequest of A. Personnaz, 1937.
**38.** Alfred Sisley: *Louveciennes. The Heights of Marly,* c. 1873.
Canvas, 0.38 × 0.46. Bequest of A. Personnaz, 1937.
**39.** Berthe Morisot (1841-1895): *In the Wheat,* 1875.
Canvas, 0.46 × 0.69. Bequest of A. Personnaz, 1937.
**40.** Alfred Sisley: *Snow at Marly-le-Roi,* 1875.
Canvas, 0.46 × 0.56. Bequest of E. Moreau-Nélaton, 1906.
**41.** Alfred Sisley: *Road at Louveciennes in the Snow,* c. 1877-1878.
Canvas, 0.46 × 0.55. Gift of Dr. and Mme A. Charpentier, 1951.
**42.** Alfred Sisley: *Snow at Louveciennes,* 1878.
Canvas, 0.61 × 0.50. Bequest of I. de Camondo, 1911.
**43.** Claude Monet: *Train in the Countryside,* c. 1870-1871.
Canvas, 0.50 × 0.65. Allocated to the Louvre by the Office des Biens privés, 1950.
**44.** Pierre-Auguste Renoir (1841-1919): *Railway Bridge at Chatou,* 1881.
Canvas, 0.54 × 0.65. Bequest of G. Caillebotte, 1894.
**45.** Pierre-Auguste Renoir: *Alfonsine Fournaise,* 1879.
Canvas, 0.73 × 0.93. Gift of D. David-Weill, 1937.
**46.** Berthe Morisot: *Butterfly Hunting,* 1874.
Canvas, 0.46 × 0.56. Gift of E. Moreau-Nélaton, 1906.
**47.** Pierre-Auguste Renoir: *Dance in the Country,* 1882-1883.
Canvas, 1.80 × 0.90. Purchased in 1979.
**48.** Claude Monet: *Landscape: The Plain at Argenteuil,* 1872.
Canvas, 0.53 × 0.72. Allocated to the Louvre by the Office des Biens privés, 1951.
**49.** Claude Monet: *Resting under the Lilas,* c. 1873.
Canvas, 0.50 × 0.65. Gift of E. Moreau-Nélaton, 1906.
**50.** Claude Monet: *The Luncheon,* c. 1873.
Canvas, 1.60 × 2.01. Bequest of G. Caillebotte, 1894.
**51.** Claude Monet: *Poppies,* 1873.
Canvas, 0.50 × 0.65. Gift of E. Moreau-Nélaton, 1906.
**52.** Pierre-Auguste Renoir: *Uphill Path in Tall Grass,* c. 1876-1878.
Canvas, 0.60 × 0.74. Gift of Ch. Cormiot through the intermediary of the Société des Amis du Louvre, 1926.
**53.** Claude Monet: *The Argenteuil Basin,* 1875.
Canvas, 0.60 × 0.80. Bequest of I. de Camondo, 1911.
**54.** Alfred Sisley: *A Square in Argenteuil,* 1872.
Canvas, 0.46 × 0.66. Gift of E. Moreau-Nélaton, 1906.

**55.** Claude Monet: *A Barnyard in Normandy,* c. 1864.
Canvas, 0.65 × 0.81. Bequest of M. and Mme R. Koechlin, 1931.
**56.** Claude Monet: *Flowering Garden,* c. 1866.
Canvas, 0.65 × 0.54. Allocated to the Louvre by the Office des Biens privés, 1950.
**57.** Claude Monet: *The Magpie,* 1868-1869.
Canvas, 0.89 × 1.30. Purchased in 1984.
**58.** Claude Monet: *The Cart. Snow-Covered Road in Honfleur,* c. 1867.
Canvas, 0.65 × 0.92. Bequest of I. de Camondo, 1911.
**59.** Claude Monet: *Vétheuil Church, Snow,* 1879.
Canvas, 0.65 × 0.50. Gift of M. and R. Kaganovitch, 1973.
**60.** Camille Pissarro: *Snow at Eragny,* 1894.
Canvas, 0.73 × 0.92. Bequest of I. de Camondo, 1911.
**61.** Camille Pissarro: *Landscape: Church and Farm at Eragny,* 1895.
Canvas, 0.60 × 0.73. Bequest of A. Personnaz, 1937.
**62.** Camille Pissarro: *Woman in a Field, Spring Sun, Eragny,* 1887.
Canvas, 0.54 × 0.65. Bequest of A. Personnaz, 1937.
**63.** Camille Pissarro: *Harvest Time at Montfoucault,* 1876.
Canvas, 0,65 × 0.92. Bequest of G. Caillebotte, 1894.
**64.** Paul Gauguin (1848-1903): *Haymaking Time in Brittany,* 1888.
Canvas, 0.73 × 0.92. Bequest of P. Jamot, 1941.
**65.** Claude Monet: *Grainstacks, End of Summer, Morning,* 1890.
Canvas, 0.60 × 1.00. Purchased in 1975.
**66.** Paul Gauguin: *Golden Grainstacks,* 1889.
Canvas, 0.73 × 0.92. Gift of Mme Huc de Monfreid, 1951.
**67.** Paul Sérusier (1863-1927): *Fence in Bloom,* 1889.
Canvas, 0.72 × 0.60. Purchased in 1980.
**68.** Émile Bernard (1868-1841): *Madeleine in the Bois d'Amour,* 1888.
Canvas, 1.37 × 1.64. Purchased in 1977.
**69.** Paul Gauguin: *Brittany Landscape, David Mill,* 1894.
Canvas, 0.73 × 0.92. Formerly in the Matsukata Collection; allocated to the Louvre according to the terms of the 1859. Peace Treaty with Japan.
**70.** Paul Sérusier: *The Talisman,* 1888.
Wood, 0.27 × 0.21. Purchased in 1985 with the generous aid of M. P.M., transmitted by the Fondation Lutèce.
**71.** Paul Gauguin: *The Roman Burial Ground of Arles,* 1888.
Canvas, 0.91 × 0.72. Gift of Countess Vitali in memory of her brother Viscount G. de Cholet, 1923.
**71.** Vincent van Gogh: *Church in Auvers,* 1890.
Canvas, 0.94 × 0.74. Purchased with the aid of P. Gachet and an anonymous Canadian donation, 1951.
**73.** Vincent van Gogh: *Doctor Gachet's Garden,* 1890.
Canvas, 0.73 × 0.52. Gift of P. Gachet, 1954.
**74.** Maurice de Vlaminck (1876-1958): *Restaurant at Marly-le-Roi,* c. 1905.
Canvas, 0.60 × 0.81. Gift of M. and R. Kaganovitch, 1973.
**75.** Paul Cézanne: *Rocks near the Caves above Château-Noir,* c. 1904.
Canvas, 0.65 × 0.54. Acquired in payment of inheritance taxes, 1978.
**76.** Georges Seurat (1859-1891): *Edge of the Woods in Spring,* c. 1882.
Wood, 0.16 × 0.26. Gift of M. and R. Kaganovitch, 1973.
**77.** Henri-Edmond Cross (1856-1910): *Cypress Trees at Cagnes,* 1908.
Canvas, 0.80 × 1.00. Bequest of G. de Cholet, 1923.
**78.** Claude Monet: *Monet's Garden at Giverny,* 1900.
Canvas, 0.81 × 0.92. Acquired in payement of inheritance taxes, 1983.
**79.** Pierre Bonnard (1867-1947): *The Big Garden,* 1898.
Canvas, 1.68 × 2.20. Gift of M. J.-Cl. Bellier in memory of his father Raph Bellier, 1982.
**80.** Gustave Klimt (1862-1918): *Rosebushes under Trees,* c. 1905.
Canvas, 1.10 × 1.10. Purchased in 1980.